A SCREAMING BLAST

A SCREAMING BLAST

EXCEPTIONAL ENTERTAINING

Rebecca Gardner

OF HOUSES & PARTIES

FOREWORD BY SOFIA COPPOLA

RIZZOLI
NEW YORK

New York · Paris · London · Milan

Contents

FOREWORD
By Sofia Coppola

My dream would be to have Rebecca Gardner

in charge of the party committee of my life. Her taste, creativity, eye for beauty, and sense of fun mean so much to me. When I'm stressed from work, I look at her fanciful tablescapes and the beautiful tableware she finds, and my blood pressure drops.

I will never forget the most beautiful party she did for my birthday in our garden under glowing lanterns, with pink ruffled tablecloths, buckets of champagne, exploding peonies, and silver baskets of lychees. With an eye for detail, the elegance of a hostess from a bygone era, and always up for some mischievous fun, Rebecca knows how to do it!

Now more than ever, we are all needing some beauty and effervescence, and these images give a lift and let you fall into the rosy lens of Rebecca's world. They make you remember to surround yourself with what inspires you and make time to create a setting to get people together that you love.

I will enjoy poring over these pages, with my beautiful Granduca mug from her shop, Houses & Parties, taking inspiration and imagining how it can be done!

Drumroll, Please

I grew up in South Texas, a Technicolor dreamscape defined by independence, cowboys, Tejano music, and hurricanes. The subtropical landscape hovered around 110 degrees, the humidity around 78 percent. Good for skin, bad for hair. The world I knew was hugely social, and not for show. Gathering was a ritual and a lifeline.

Both of my parents were from South Texas. But everyone had Mississippi Delta roots. These distinctive party places are known for lively music, delicious food, and a good time. My paternal grandmother, Neely Gardner, ran a beautiful house and entertained almost every week. I treasure my stack of Nee-Nee's desk calendars, filled with reminders to pick basil for Roquefort biscuits, send flowers for birthdays, gather for dinners with friends, and celebrate those birthdays later in the week. All mixed with a shocking number of hairstyling appointments.

It was not all white gloves and gardenias. When she was a teenager, Nee-Nee's banker father died by suicide after a string of failed business prospects. Her mother, Annie Proctor, suddenly responsible for her family's livelihood, leaned into her own areas of expertise: parties and people. She started a catering business in Houston. I remember photos of the cake she baked for my grandparents' wedding at home, but I didn't realize the scope of her business until I was unpacking storage boxes a few years ago. It was all there, including Annie's receipts from 1947 for butter and sugar and photos of her impressive staff lined up on the front lawn.

Long before oversize kitchens were in vogue, Nee-Nee's snappy mid-century modern ranch had a double oven and a place for everything: molds shaped like a lamb for Easter and a jumping fish for salmon mousse, scalloped for tomato aspic and tiny scalloped for individual tomato aspics; graters with big holes for giant blocks of sharp cheddar, medium holes for lime zest, and micro holes for nutmeg; and cast-iron pans for cornbread, copper pans for sauces, nonstick pans for omelets, and custom pans made for buckwheat blinis just right for a generous dollop of caviar. An entire wall of floor-to-ceiling cabinets lined in felt held dinner services for eighteen, from matching butter pads to tureens. Another wall of cabinets was lined with Silvercloth.

Nee-Nee was a shopper. Perhaps this was an instinctive response to the want of her youth. She designed her house specifically for entertaining. I spent an inordinate amount of time there, spoiled with attention and activity. I set the table in the dining room, peeled figs for preserves, watered plant specimens in the greenhouse, and danced to Judi Sheppard Missett Jazzercise videos. I vividly remember an electric plate warmer and how, while the adults had cocktails, I'd slip my hands into its blanket pockets and pretend I was having a paraffin wax treatment. Nee-Nee's house was kept up with an old-fashioned formality—everything ironed and polished and ready to share. Her attention to hospitality, even for intimate family, had a monumental impact on how I define comfort and elegance and generosity and home.

The main fridge was stocked with everyday sundries like a grocery store, while the extra three freezers in the utility room held my grandfather's game: venison loin, redfish fillets, and bobwhite quail. He taught me how to fillet a fish, and saved their eyeballs in spice jars for my seventh-grade science class.

My grandfather Big Joe was a gentleman of the Greatest Generation. He was a radiologist, a graduate of the University of Mississippi and Tulane medical school, and our favorite game was a challenge of unconditional love. I'd invent wildly imaginative and wicked scenes in which I was the culprit. They involved greed and wrath and envy and gluttony and sloth and a nose ring. Then, I'd ask if he would still love me. His answer was always yes.

He was famous for his Delta drawl, wicked sense of humor, complete lack of pretension, and tequila sours. When I unpacked his things from storage, amid the muddlers, stirrers, Louis Armstrong records, and mushed Lester Lanin hats, I found a file of X-rays he had made of my grandmother's orchids.

I spent my childhood watching two people like a hawk—Kristi Yamaguchi and Uncle Bill. Uncle Bill, my father's brother, lived in Los Angeles, Houston, and, for a flash, Corpus Christi, where he owned a floral shop with a giant walk-in cooler stocked with a four-gallon water dispenser full of bourbon milk punch. When my brother and I were children, he punctuated our holidays with eye-popping, toe-curling gifts from his buying trips to Europe. He's now a venerable antiques dealer. There were tins of pâté from the South of France and Prada cosmetic bags likely bought on the fly at the Milan Malpensa duty-free.

Uncle Bill still loves going inside the bank to do business. This blows my mind, but I do appreciate the newly minted cash that he rolls in wads like a drug dealer and ties with French wired ribbon to give my brother and me at Christmas. He once sent us to Spain with a roll, and required that we bring back all our receipts to prove we spent his money solely on joy.

It was all part of his plan to entertain us—and to antagonize my parents. One Easter, my dad found a giant chicken-wire-and-bamboo cage spray-painted hot pink and filled with pastel paper grass in our driveway.

A white bunny with bubblegum ears was nesting inside. I named her Sadie, and she grew at an incredible rate until she was so big that Big Joe had to build a hutch next to our house. She was not affectionate or playful, and she bit us with resentment in her beady pink eyes. Eventually, Sadie gave birth to ten little Sadies.

Uncle Bill is the single most creative person I have ever met. He is an encyclopedia of art and design history and offers a never-ending list of obscure references and directives. He gives me ideas and boosts and stories and kindness and family and home . . . but never patience.

This book is dedicated to my Uncle Bill.

RIDE THAT TRAIN (EVERYBODY)

Sometimes the change of season is reason enough to celebrate; it certainly is in Oakville, California, where September marks the annual grape harvest and a fellow good-timer happens to have a house right on the route of the Napa Valley Wine Train.

The 1910 Sears Modern Home is called "Petticoat Junction," and it is a kicked-back, colorful, Ken Fulk–decorated, joy-maker. We pulled all the straw hats and wicker rockers onto the porch, poured hefty margaritas, and gave everyone an ice breaking with a celebrity face for fodder. Then a brass band led guests in a second line to dinner. All this just as the train passed by amid plenty of hooting and hollering.

The tables were set with the last of fall's fat dahlias, and tiny ceramic snails explored a bounty of fruit from the local market. Notice how the garland, made of torn rags in the happiest colors, hangs low over the tables. This tops a little world made just for this memorable occasion.

CAVIAR & SAMOVAR

Parties are no place for minimalism. There is celebration in excess. The evening began by passing through an inconspicuous door in New York's Theater District. A Liberace look-alike with rings on all his fingers greeted guests. The delicious thunder of laughter over icy vodka was muffled only by a red velvet curtain that separated the long hallway from a luscious, seated dinner.

Tables were nestled into red leather banquettes, and Miss Hannigan lampshades hung low and cozy, their rayon fringe tickling the tallest guests. Shades of red ranunculus and gloriosa lilies reached across tables draped in Pavlovo Posad shawls. The ruffled linen napkins looked like Mr. Showmanship's blouse.

After dinner, animated folk dancers whished around tables banging their tambourines and demanding the party move upstairs for a giant croquembouche, pomegranate-infused vodka, and New York City Ballet prima ballerinas prancing on pedestals alongside the DJ. There are a few insider marks of a successful party; a grande dame wearing a foam beehive is number one.

BIRDS OF A FEATHER

A "Map to Matrimony" marked the spots for a destination wedding weekend in Napa, taking the "Path of Pleasures" into the "Forest through the Trees" to the "County of Compromise."

Guests wound their way through a flock of lovebirds nesting in the rose garden inspired by a favorite Tim Walker photograph. After the ceremony, dinner was served under a vine-covered pergola. Low-hanging lanterns and tumbling table arrangements showcased the agrarian abundance of the region and the season.

Butterflies danced in bubbles, and just about everyone wore a late-night costume—testament to the importance of your guest list. The bride stepped on a piece of glass, doused the cut with vodka, threw a mylar eyelash jacket over her shoulders, and jumped on the party bus headed to a silent disco.

Fortune Favors the Bold

Growing up, the most fabulous party I knew was hosted by my godparents, Lica and Marc. Their annual Easter celebration started with a three-hour trek across the border to Nuevo Laredo. Always several families, always in Suburbans, always very hot. In Mexico, we'd spend hours at the market eyeing silver puff heart earrings and begging our mothers for counterfeit Dooney & Bourke bucket bags. Negotiation was easy, as long as we agreed to carry the giant Easter piñata back across the border and amuse ourselves while they dove into lethal margaritas at the Cadillac Bar.

One year, back at the party, a suspiciously cheerful Peter Rabbit piñata in a pink Eton suit caused a stir when it turned out to be lined and stuffed with Mexican pornography. The women screamed while the men scrambled to gather bits of bosom.

I ignored the children who sat in the garage and gnawed on cold drumsticks and snuck into the formal dining room to steal beef tenderloin on a yeast roll and stare at the oil painting of Lica's beautiful mother. She had a house in Watch Hill.

South Texas has its own brand of unlikely panache. It would be years before I knew of Marella Agnelli, but I sure knew all about Aqua Net and Lynn Wyatt, Sue Ellen Ewing, and Mrs. Kroeger, my best friend's mom, who had a walnut-paneled living room full of Fortuny.

Every year on my birthday, my mother "knocked herself out." Thanks to the pictures and constant reminders of her effort, my memories of childhood are still organized by party.

One year, lunch was served in straw cowboy hats turned upside down like baskets. We sat on quilts on the lawn, surrounded by pots of pink impatiens planted expressly for the event. Another year, a stylish local newscaster emceed a fashion show, and I was the last to walk the paved runway—also the driveway—dressed as the bride in ecru polyester. When I turned thirteen, there was a deejayed dance, remarkably bare until a courier arrived with an embarrassment of birds-of-paradise and orchids shooting out of cored pineapples, courtesy of Uncle Bill. Needless to say, I've never had a party at a ball pit.

As a child, I told my teenage cousin that if she didn't let me have one of the Rice Krispies Treats cooling on the stovetop, I wouldn't—pause for thought—invite her to my party. It was the harshest punishment I could fathom, at four or at forty.

From ages six to sixteen, I attended a girls-only summer camp in the Texas Hill Country. I shunned the brutality of six a.m. War Canoe and stayed in the shade, making arts and crafts and care packages for any cabinmate who might have lost a tennis match. Later I pretended to hate camp, leading my cabin in a rendition of "Hotel California" with lyrics reworked to stage a coup against a synchronized swimming routine planned for parents' weekend. The truth is, camp rituals formed me. The cypress trees, with their massive trunks and lacy leaves, threw delicate, patchy light on the Guadalupe River like fairy dust. There was reveille over a speaker at the start of each day and silent, starry darkness each night, broken only by the sound of a bugle playing taps and every girl in camp calling out in unison to wish each other goodnight. Summer camp taught me the indelible magic of an environment informed not by whims and wants, but instead by a visceral sense of what people need: a tribe, a campfire, a sing-along.

In high school I partied like everyone else I knew. I drank beer, smoked Parliament Lights, and tapped my tasseled loafers to Coolio. I spent Friday nights driving with my friends up and down the street, looking to see whose parents were out of town.

I don't remember a single class at Ole Miss, but I remember all my parties. I roomed with a friend from camp, and before football games we invited everyone for a toast, drinking cheap champagne from Styrofoam cups with curlers in our hair. Loads of remarkable musicians came through Oxford, many on a blues pilgrimage to see the crossroads where Robert Johnson sold his soul to the devil; others were local legends. So, we had the undeserved privilege of dancing to, for example, T-Model Ford on the back deck of a fraternity house. This is the education I remember.

As a consolation prize for my parents' divorce (and, officially, so I could focus on my studies), I lived by myself at the Flamingo Arms, a glamorous pink stucco Art Deco apartment building crowned by a wrought iron brackish bird. My true focus was entertaining friends visiting from the University of Texas and just about anyone who stayed for summer school.

The best party I threw at the Flamingo was inspired by the beloved late-night egg rolls from the Chevron gas station across the street. I drove around with my friend Kathleen and a serrated bread knife, cutting down bamboo so tall we had to slide it into my car diagonally through open windows and slouch down in our seats to get home. I lined my entire living room and dining room with bamboo stalks and bunched kudzu around the bottom for effect. The most sophisticated thing I could think to make was a loose interpretation of P. F. Chang's lettuce wraps. A glassy-eyed sorority sister wandered into my kitchen holding an empty iceberg shell and asked me for "more meat." "We should have gone to Washington and Lee," Kathleen declared.

During childhood and adolescence, when almost everything felt beyond my control, parties were a salve. Sometimes the answers are already there, and it's just up to you to make it happen.

ALIEN BALLOON WORLD

The solution for a cavernous space at a contemporary art gallery in downtown Los Angeles was a superscale alien balloon world. This was my chance to work with multidisciplinary artist Jason Hackenwerth. Excitement gathered as guests walked under the bellies of these looming creatures and into our lair.

The tables were dressed in waxed cotton Ankara prints and a playful assemblage of gerbera daisies, chrysanthemums, strings of cherry tomatoes, and totems of watermelon radishes.

After dinner, toasts, and roasts, the string lights went dim and the DJ burst from the belly of a balloon creature with an accompanying light show. Every guest was glued to the dance floor, breaking only to refuel at an ice cream truck.

SALLY

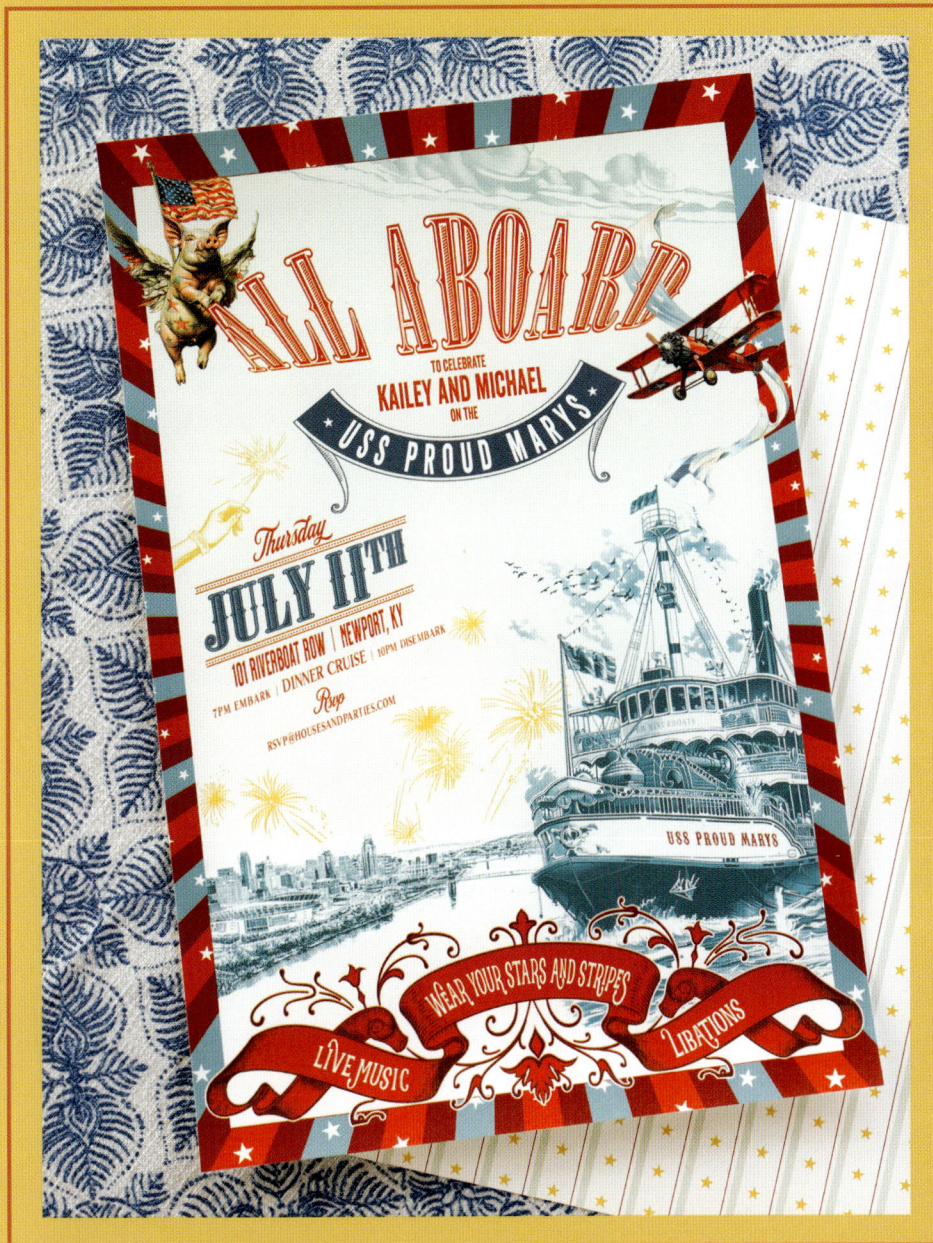

ROLLING ON THE RIVER

There is a lovely charm to a hometown wedding and a surprising novelty to tourist entertainments that locals take for granted. For the welcome party, we repurposed a Cincinnati riverboat into the USS *Proud Marys* in honor of the bride's and groom's mothers, who share the name.

Guests explored the gigantic boat and its offerings—a rock band, corn dogs, and caricatures. We served bourbon slushies to ensure everyone was Rolling on the River.

Having at least three happenings at every party keeps the rhythm of surprise. First, a Cessna circled low around the boat, trailing a banner for the bride and groom. Then, as guests gathered on the stern to watch the sunset, a neighboring pontoon boat barreled toward them. Everyone screamed and waved their hands, warning of an impending collision. Blasting Creedence Clearwater Revival, the pirates waved gigantic cutouts of the bride's and groom's faces—and mooned the entire party. Indecorous. Indecent. Incredibly fun. It all ended with a monumental display of fireworks near the Roebling Bridge.

Forced Serendipity

My first job was hugely influential, with a precocious title to match: Director of Creative Initiatives at the Savannah College of Art and Design (SCAD), a university with campuses in Savannah, Atlanta, the South of France, and, at the time, Hong Kong. My responsibilities were many and more. At twenty-three years old, I bought art, entertained swishy names, and decorated a medieval château in the Luberon Valley. Looking back, I can see the gifts of the place more clearly—unbounded possibility and killer resources, for starters. The school's president and founder, Paula Wallace, saw something in me that I didn't see in myself. She once introduced me as her protégé, and I grew twelve inches. Inspired by her incredible focus and tenacity, I gladly dedicated almost a decade to building and creating, leaving only when I was worn by the whims of the weather.

At SCAD, I met movers and shakers in the world of art and design. I organized dinners for Frank Gehry and decorated luncheons for Tom Ford. I carried the conversation at a dinner with Philippe de Montebello where no one else seemed to have anything to say. I learned about the relentless pursuit of excellence and that you must plan fun rather than wait for it to happen.

Contrary to how it sounds, forced serendipity is a great kindness to your guests. As a host, you're the director, and the care you take will be felt by everyone in attendance.

Always state a purpose for the evening, and if there isn't one, make it up. There is always a reason to celebrate. A theme party to honor your favorite TV series. A block party to welcome a new neighbor. An alfresco luncheon to celebrate blooming irises. I happen to love costume directives, but no matter what, the host must dress the part, passing cocktails and compliments with equal abandon. Even if it requires an Academy Award–worthy performance, act at ease and remember that you're in charge. Your timeline. Your menu. Your vices. Your people. Make strategic introductions and ask thoughtful questions. Please invite someone different from your regular crowd; the best gift you can give your guests is a new friend.

At every party, big or small, the host has ultimate influence, and for control freaks like me, it comes as a huge relief to decide how the night will unfold. Whether I want everyone to leave at nine or to leave their Spanx under the powder room sink, I can create an atmosphere and energy that steers the night toward a particular port of call. Intention is everything, and your choices—be they white-jacketed waiters or bountiful platters passed family style—will show people how you want them to feel.

For a seated dinner, placement is crucial. Remember that hosting is, above all, an act of generosity. It's incumbent upon you to create a little world for your guests: twenty-four inches expressly intended for them, bookended by two opportunities for excellent conversation. You can go on and on and on with decorations, but I think flattering light and heavy pours are much more important. Plan like Patton to decrease your margin of error and then at some point, as they say in Alabama, "Let go and let God." Effort is the key. Effortless is the look.

Your guests may not remember the boring white box during Fashion Week, but they'll never forget the burlesque dancers crawling out from under the tables after dessert has been cleared—especially not if you look as shocked as they feel. The dancers may have been hiding for an hour and a half, but that's showbiz.

I once hired a saxophone player to laze against a tree in Savannah's Forsyth Park playing "Moon River" and then pretended not to know him.

For a wedding in a once-derelict sausage factory with several balconies, we passed out little rings holding a bell and a sachet of tightly wound (and secretly extra-long) crepe paper.

At "you may now kiss the bride," guests let their streamers fly, and we all saw at once what two hundred, thirty-foot streamers look like cascading down three stories.

A blonde Southern bride marrying into a massive New York Italian family wanted to honor her in-laws with a splash, and so as the reception drew to a close, we zipped her into a Dolce & Gabbana sheath and plopped a Sophia Loren wig on her head. The servers wheeled her out onto the dance floor surrounded by platters of Italian wedding cookies and boxes of heart-shaped pizza. It was an epic ode to crossing over, even if no one recognized her.

For the first dinner party I ever threw as an independent, employed adult, I took a whole Friday off work to get ready. The menu featured chateaubriand, mushroom soufflé, and asparagus vichyssoise. My first and last creamy Julia Child moment. When the potatoes were peeled and the tenderloin was resting, I trekked to the florist to spend a fortune on peonies. I printed songbooks filled with Christmas carols and superimposed my guests' faces on dancing elves, and the run of show was savage: every song meant the next course was served. My guests had to sing for their supper. I remember thinking it was a good way to incentivize some in the group who might otherwise retreat. In any case, we had a ball, ending our evening ecstatically drunk, tossing handfuls of exorbitant flowers into the air and passing beers out the window to affable passersby.

This party cemented the maxim that the success of an evening is marked by the enthusiasm of the final sing-along. When I moved six years later, I found peony petals pressed under my sisal rug.

ASPEN PARTY ANIMALS

Friends came from far and wide to celebrate her fortieth birthday. The directive was clear: Party animals, have a good time. Civilized cocktails came to an abrupt halt with a drumroll. The party parade traveled down the hill with banners, tambourines, and crazy fringed capes while the trumpeter played a medley that stretched from "Louie Louie" to Ginuwine.

Down the rabbit hole, into the valley, through arches of aspen branches, among Glastonbury-ish flags. Guests made their way to the tent draped with yards of red and pink shantung and strung with garland made from favorite fabric memos—Décors Barbares to Donghia.

Merriments included a chicken-carving competition, senior-superlative awards, and ice-cream sundaes. Back up the hill for hits of the '90s, a dance competition, a custom balloon milliner, and a campfire.

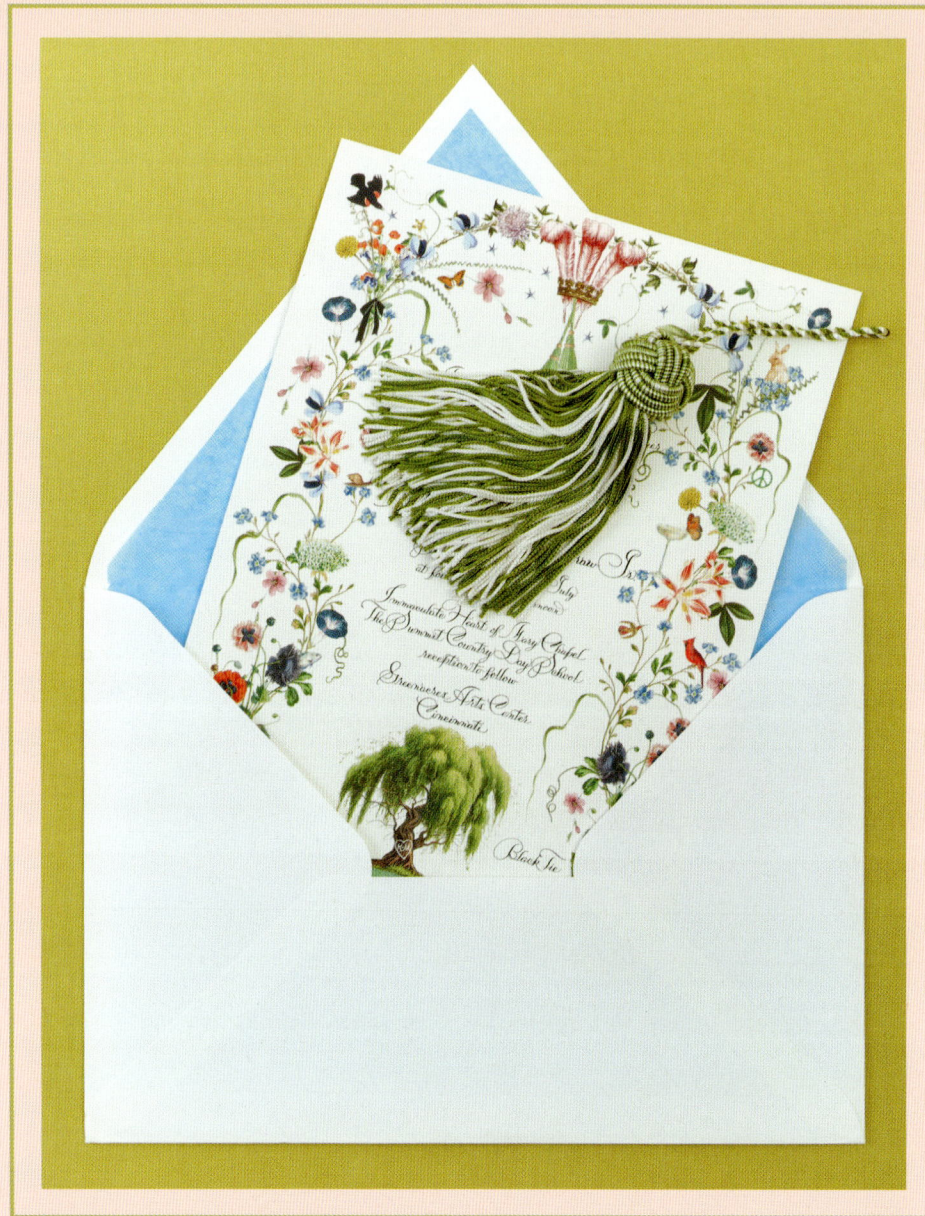

LUXE & LOOSE

We began with a fairy-tale vision at an English Norman–style manor complete with a turret, a teahouse, a cascading fountain, and a moat. A line of servers in the finest livery greeted guests with cocktails under fanciful tents bedecked with chartreuse silk tassels.

Guests made their way to dinner, passing by the fountain and under the bridge, through the installation of weeping willow, which encouraged everyone to "sha-la-la-la-la-la kiss the girl."

The ten-thousand-square-foot tent, draped in ten thousand yards of chiffon, was anchored by a twenty-four-foot-wide weeping willow from which a teensy garland made of jasmine blooms hung like strings of pearls. After dinner and the most heartfelt toasts, guests were distracted by a loud drumroll. An entire side of the tent fell to the ground, revealing an adjacent tent with an eighteen-piece band, pink and purple lamé, disco balls, and sexy chandelier dancers.

If It's Worth Doing, It's Worth Overdoing

I started my event and interiors design firm on my thirtieth birthday. Everything that followed came down to hard work. I've been a student of parties all my life, and though I'm more introverted than my profession might suggest, I'm a great guest. How to be a great guest? Bring something. A sense of humor. A great pair of legs. An infectious laugh. A dynamic story. A wild opinion. A good bottle of wine. Be more interested *in* others than you are in *impressing* others.

A note on scale: instead of a psychiatrist, I see a loving and brilliant witch doctor in Los Angeles. She has diagnosed me as a "professional exaggerator," which makes sense. I like lots of color, bold statements, big jewelry, loud music, and strong drinks. Everyone extols the virtues of low lighting, but I like lighting as dim as a panther's cave. If something is small, I like it teeny tiny. If it's big, I prefer

thirty feet. I don't grab a matchbook as I leave a restaurant, I take three. More is more—ting-tang, walla-walla, bing-bang.

When I walk a client through an event, there are three major movements: a creative brief outlining the entire party from a guest's perspective, a discussion of budget (the worst), and a run of show. Houses & Parties formalized the shift from hosting personal events to planning events for others to host, but my convictions haven't changed. They've only gotten stronger.

This is a big party. Imagine packing a house, unpacking that house, decorating that house, and then hosting a seated dinner for two hundred in that house . . . all in four days. In the mad dash to get it done, my feet take on their own heartbeat, one that rivals the groove of any drum section. When the iced coffee hits the seventh moon as I tie bow ties on a gaggle of servers with an hour to go until guests arrive, the theme from *Chariots of Fire* plays on repeat in my head.

Sometimes I creep into a corner and watch the crowd walk in, eyeballs light up and phones come out to make memories in the way we all do. Seeing everyone dance like crazy in a world that I made is a special feeling. The postmortem phone calls the next morning gild my lily-loving heart. "Find a job you love, and you'll never work a day in your life," Mark Twain said—or was it Confucius? Regardless, I'm so grateful this job is mine. When I'm at work, I plan parties. When I'm bored, I plan parties. When I'm on vacation, I plan parties. Nothing is more exciting to me than learning it's someone's birthday. I take the cake.

There is a moment during every party I've ever planned, when guests are surprised by something I've set in motion, and somehow, I'm surprised, too. I get goose bumps, and often tears follow. To be fair, I've always cried when I'm exhausted.

A few years ago, I did a wedding at a family farm for a longtime member of my team—my right hand, someone I adore. Emotions were as high as the Tennessee ryegrass we forbade the bride's father from cutting all summer. We were going for Maya Lin's *Storm King Wavefield*. The father takes a great deal of pride in his lawn, but he committed to our vision and the results were magnificent. I let out a mariachi *grito* as he rode with his daughter in a horse-drawn carriage through waving fields of grain to the ceremony. She looked back and knew just where to find me: hiding, my sweaty ponytail looking like a calligraphy brush. "I love you, Rebecca!" she yelled as she waved a loose bouquet of white cosmos, and, hand to heart, I felt the last piece click into place.

WILDFLOWERS IN THE MOONLIGHT

The bride's mother planted tens of thousands of poppies. Her father babysat the tall grass all spring and summer in preparation for our winding path. Guests rode in a covered wagon train from the road to the lakefront site.

Banjoists played "You Are My Sunshine" and a bit of Merle Haggard. I suspect her brother tipped the musician to include "Mama Tried" in the medley. I live for this mischief.

Cocktails were served in a nearby field dense with pine. We hung galvanized pails filled with longnecks from the branches. Martagon lilies seemingly grew from the shaded undergrowth in patches of color.

A giant "moon" cast light on the wildflowers that grew from the tabletops. It was fifteen feet wide and lingered inches from the floor during dinner, then it rose among the stars to signal the start of dancing. I begged the groomsmen to "hang the moon" with theatrical effort on antique pulleys that we found in a nearby barn.

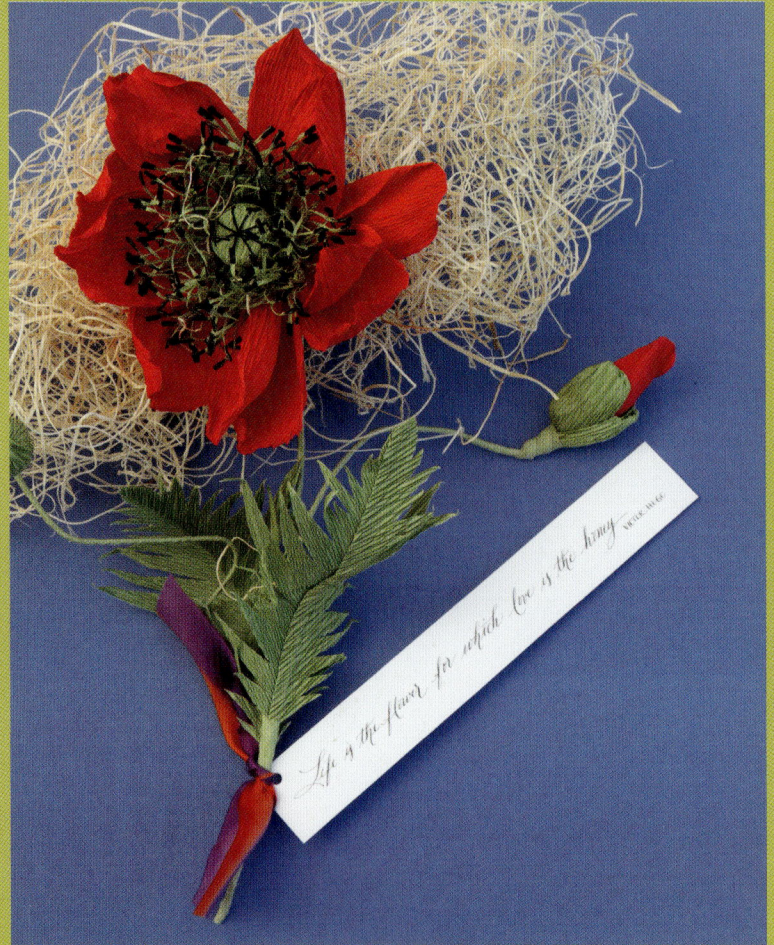

Life is the flower for which love is the honey. —VICTOR HUGO

DIOR OR DU JOUR

For my own birthday party, I mix friends from all different parts of my life, old and new. And I love a theme. This year was Dior or Du Jour. We drank in a hotel lobby, dined at a bistro next door, departed in a vintage school bus, and dallied at a raucous dueling piano bar.

Planning and executing a costume is one of my greatest pleasures. I am lucky to have many willing accomplices. Servers passed woven baskets with small baguettes that, upon second glance, were plastic trompe l'oeil coin purses containing nonessentials: a gummy, a cigarette, a small red Trish McEvoy lipstick, and lyrics to "Lady Marmalade," just in case.

A school bus with neon lights, a DJ setup, and a full bar took us from Tribeca to Midtown, only stopping once for us to serenade the Times Square crowds with a spirited rendition of "Like a Prayer."

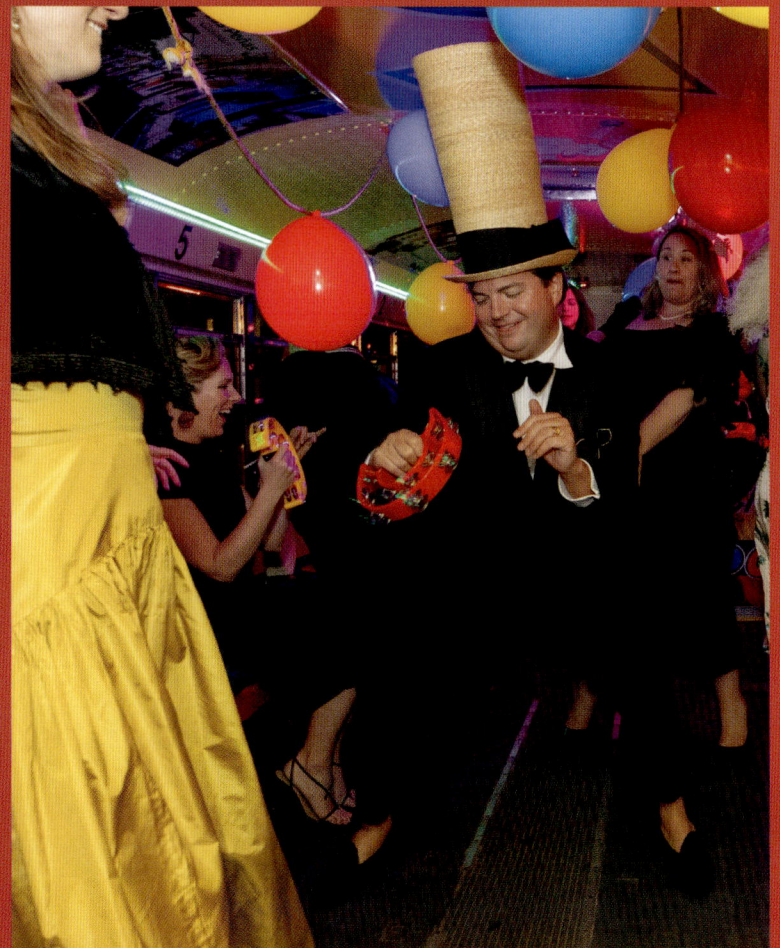

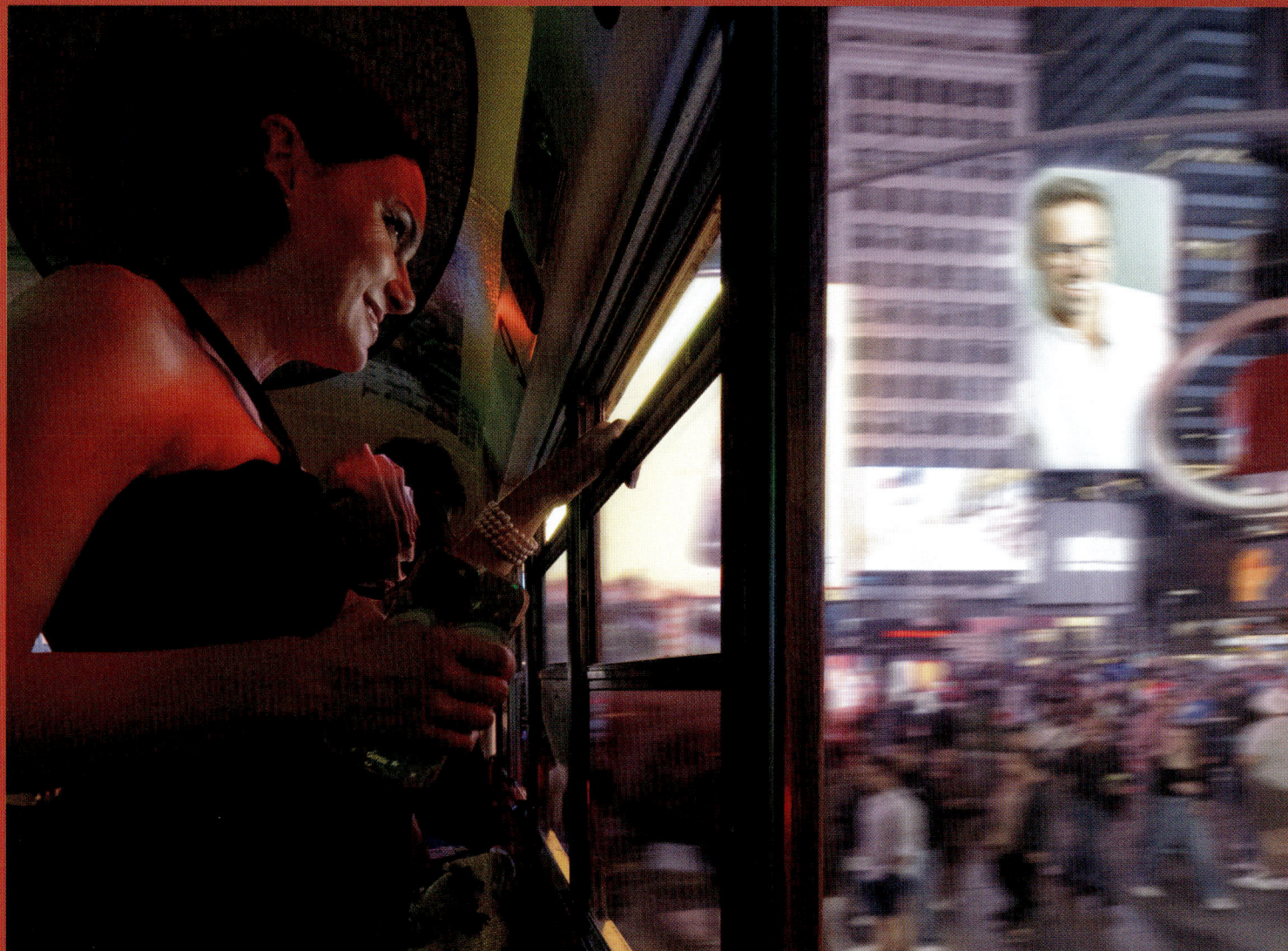

You Don't Have to Make It to Make It Happen

I make my own buttercream icing but would never think of baking a cake from scratch. Sub milk for water and melted butter for oil in a box of Duncan Hines, and no one knows the difference. If you're short on time, my country estate, Pepperidge Farm, makes a delicious coconut cake. Cakes are celebratory, and it doesn't have to be someone's birthday. I keep a plastic bin labeled "European Candy" filled with sweets I've picked up across the globe and earmarked for a cake smash.

The point is, you don't have to make it to make it happen. It's thoughtful to serve at least one thing that comes from your own kitchen, but it's no fun to be chained to the stove. Focus on what brings you joy and outsource the rest.

Remember that very dull things are flattered by fine company—elegant goes with tacky and expensive with cheap. I warn you to stay clear of the middle.

When you're deciding on a menu—and I'm cribbing from my guru, author and celebrated hostess Julia Reed—be sure to serve people something delicious. To me that means lots of colorful, fresh choices for picky eaters, a substantial protein, a sinful starch (cheesy and buttery), and a monumental dessert. No one needs dessert, which is the perfect reason to go big. I love a giant tiered cake with a million long candles, bananas Foster set aflame like you're at Brennan's, a croquembouche in a spun-sugar cage—if dessert needs to be wheeled out on a table of its own, even better. Blow their hair back.

Here, in no particular order, are foods that people like to eat: Caviar. Gulf shrimp. Roasted chicken. Beef tenderloin. Domino's thin-crust pepperoni pizza. Mr. Chow's Crispy Beef. Potpie. Roasted vegetables. Squash casserole. Green bean vinaigrette. Little gem salad. Peppermint ice cream with chocolate sauce. Tarte Tatin. Strawberries with cream. Brandy Alexander.

Skip signature cocktails and, no matter what, forget canapés. They're complicated and stinky, appetite-ruining, and rarely eaten in one bite. Small salty bar bites like cheese straws and nuts are perfectly fine, but to be left clinging to a slimy shred of smoked salmon on a crescent of cucumber is my idea of hell. I shudder to think of trays with shadows of condensation from dearly departed mini crab cakes—and don't get me started on communal dips. While we're at it, chardonnay gives you bad breath, which is why, after too many youthful misadventures, I'm ABC: Anything But Chardonnay.

I don't like the color blue, not for interiors or flowers and certainly not for food or drinks. I like warm colors, warm food, warm people. A person who is comfortable and welcoming will always attract admirers. I'm all in on pink silk moiré taffeta, and I happen to think there's a shade of red that works for everyone. Feel free to make your own rules—except about the canapés.

A note on shipping: keep your mailman at the top of your holiday gift list. You'll need those iced cookies from Brooklyn and the wine from Napa and the flowers from Amsterdam. I've driven all over town chasing the UPS truck, and I have an unusually

intimate relationship with the FedEx man, who gets a love note and homemade sugar cookies every December. Through a cousin of a friend of a friend in Memphis, I tracked down a VIP concierge contact at one of the aforementioned shippers, and now on the rarest and most frantic occasions, I dial it like the Batphone. Invariably, they ask if I'm shipping for a celebrity, and I hear myself answer, "Absolutely."

MOD SQUAD

Stylish restaurants can be excellent party venues. This mid-century gas station turned neighborhood eatery dictated the nostalgic vibe for a birthday girl born in the '50s.

It was a successful surprise: Twiggy look-alikes stood at the entrance, gathering guests in the side garden for a big reveal. We passed martinis and pigs in a blanket on pink elephant cocktail napkins while the top hits of the time drifted beyond.

Dinner was served on the covered patio. The entrance to the restaurant was restyled as an after-dinner disco den. I much prefer a big basic sheet cake from a local bakery to anything fancy and fondant. Pink piping and relighting candles spark smiles.

RUTH

CELEBRATES
RUTH

JUMBO LUMP CRAB CAKE
CREOLE MUSTARD CREME, CELERY SLAW

VEAL MILANESE
ARTICHOKE, ARUGULA, CHERRY TOMATOES

FRENCH FRIES

AND AFTERWARDS

BIRTHDAY CAKE & DANCING

THESE ENTERTAINMENTS

SATURDAY THE TWENTY FIRST OF OCTOBER
TWO THOUSAND TWENTY THREE

HOUSTON

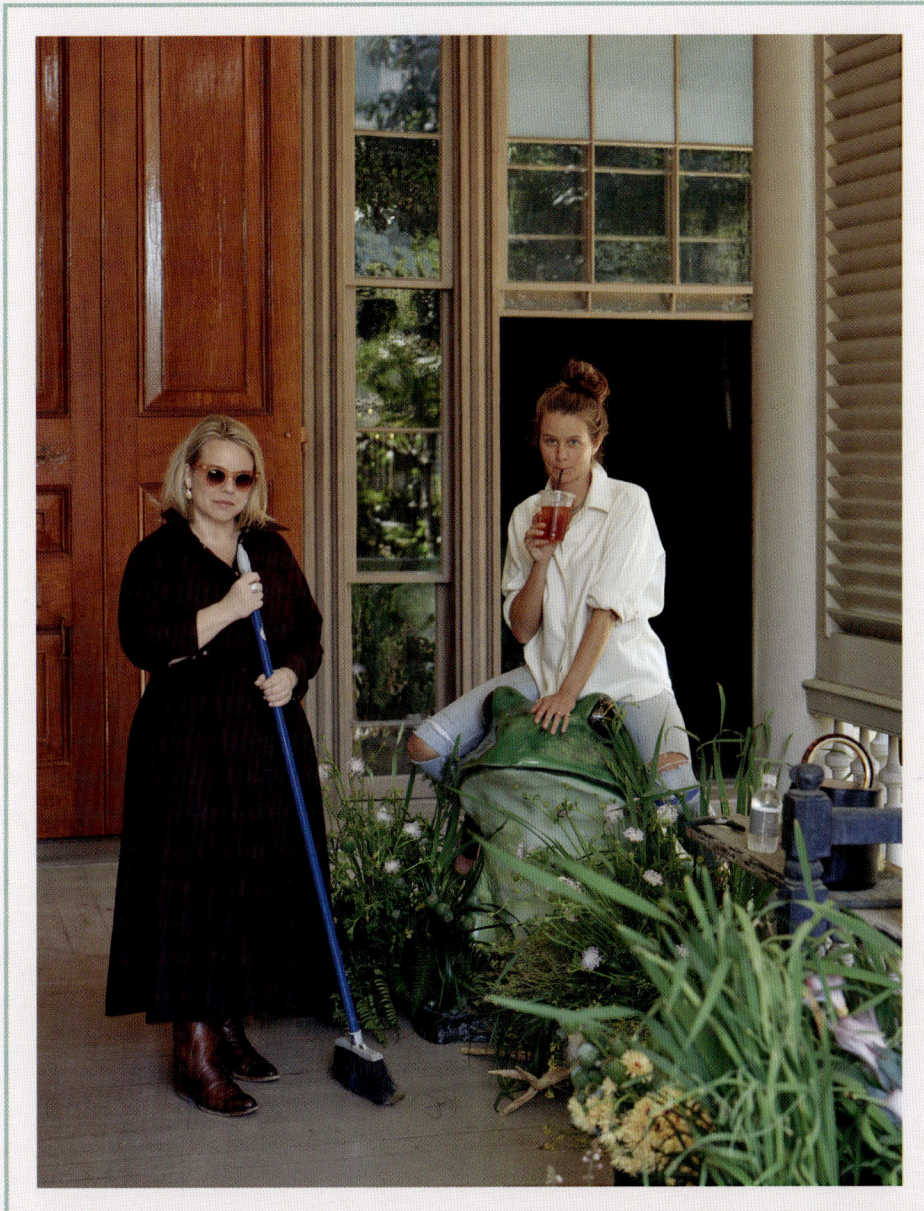

FROGS IN YONDER POND

When you wish upon a star, dinner is served at the historic Aiken-Rhett House in downtown Charleston. We showed our appreciation with hundreds of yards of tulle in three shades of green—twenty-four layers to be exact—which protected the table original to the house.

Taylor Patterson of Fox Fodder Farm fame flew down to forage palmetto and marsh grasses from the side of US 17. Each of the fiberglass toads was ready for a kiss, on individual islands of mischief.

When your service is slow, blame the snails who pass port after dinner and the princess in the corner who lifts eyebrows—but never a finger.

THE SQUIRREL CLUB

My client wanted a soiree with strong drinks, endless dancing, and unabashed fun. After scouting several dive bars and one notoriously raunchy "lounge," we landed on, unremarkably, a private club. But here's the thing: She's known for her love of squirrels, and—when given a morsel of bizarre—I yearn for more. So, the party became known as the "Squirrel Club" complete with a coat of arms.

Waitresses with long legs and fluffy tails welcomed guests as Animal Planet sounds of squirrels in the forest played throughout the entrance. We replaced the soft white lightbulbs with red, which cast a saucy glow.

Even the bartenders were up to nuttin' but trouble. Dressed in their branded coats and wearing fake front squirrel teeth, they tended to kilos of caviar. After an assistant misplaced the custom matchbooks, she made up for it at the last minute by dressing up as a furry mascot and leading guests, to my mock horror, in the "Macarena."

Something to Talk About

It's fun to gather friends and add interesting people to the mix, but hosting comes with the great responsibility of making everyone comfortable. Popularity, fame, and confidence be damned — people who don't know each other need an introduction and an icebreaker. Remember how it feels to be the stranger. Party hats, masks, and costumes are the pop and fizz that will linger long after the hangover fades. A party should always aim to entertain rather than impress. If you're worried about impressing people, your party is already lame.

One time I satisfied a request for out-of-this-world late-night entertainment by asking a mariachi band to dress up as sexy aliens.

At an engagement party on the banks of the Wilmington River, a synchronized-swimming Esther Williams routine felt too on the nose until partygoers got close enough to see that the saltwater pool was full of baby sharks, which had been supplied by local shrimpers.

For a party in Mrs. Astor's library at the St. Regis, flowers "grew" from piles of dirt on the table (to the horror of the hotel staff) and hand-painted butterflies fluttered overhead.

At a dinner during the Round Top Antiques Fair, guests made their way to tables through a foot of wood shavings I'd dumped on the floor near a 1910 Barnum & Bailey Circus caravan, towed all the way from Tennessee to Texas.

For one of my birthday parties, servers passed out plastic trompe l'oeil dinner-roll coin purses stuffed with edibles and a tiny printout with the lyrics to "Lady Marmalade," just in case there was a lull.

Lagniappe is a Cajun word meaning an unexpected extra, given or obtained gratuitously. To me, it's the crunchy bits at the bottom of a bag of fried shrimp. I dress a table, step back, contemplate, and then add the lagniappe. The lagniappe surprises and delights.

Here are a few things that will help you get the party going: Party crackers with competitive party games. Nostalgic tin windup toys that you can race for cash prizes. Lottery tickets. Erotic porcelain figurines. A boa made of dollar bills. This or That place cards (Love or Money? Leather or Lace?). A cigarette-girl bolero filled with peppermints. Oversize buttons labeling the wearer as a "lightweight," "lush," "gossip," or—gasp—"vegan."

These three words offer great value and protection: one night only. Life can be oatmeal mush, but a party is a chance to seek and find sweet relief. Think about Dennis Quaid whirling Julia Roberts around the dance floor. He cheated. She caught him. He's sorry. She's humiliated. It'll all still be there tomorrow—but tonight, they dance.

My mother's party trick when things got too polite was to smear chocolate on her teeth and walk around talking to people as if she didn't know it was there. The irony is that I spent my childhood wishing I was a grown-up, and now I've made a career out of looking all the way back with gusto.

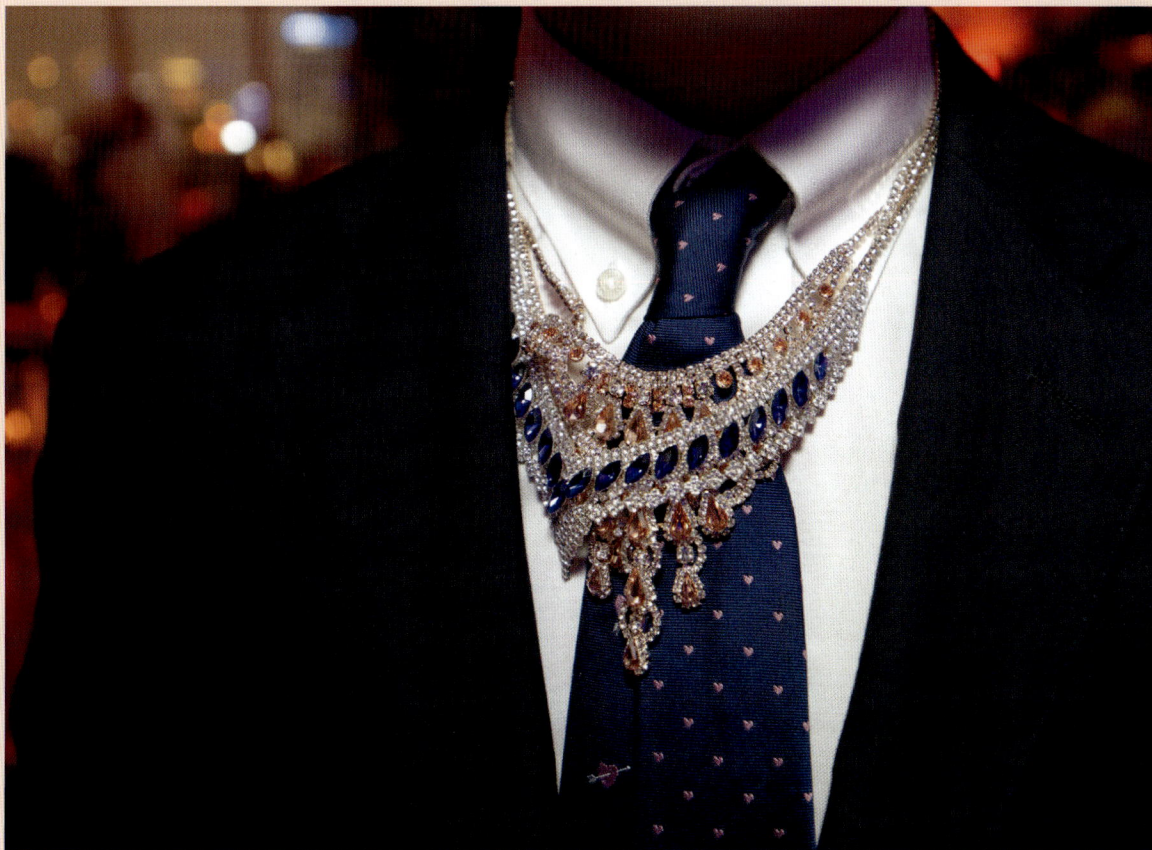

MIAMI VICES

Miami is a city built for pleasure. The party unfolded in Brickell at a forgotten club with a fabulous balcony overlooking a dance floor surrounded by banquette seating. Cocktails began upstairs. A trio in guayaberas played traditional Cuban music as guests sipped on mojitos—civilized, elegant, a teaser.

Suddenly, the dance floor below came to life. Beams of neon light shot across palm trees and landed on dining tables. Disco balls sparkled, casting dappled fairy dust, and lively music called guests to action.

The tables were set with leopard napkins on leopard cloths against leopard banquettes in front of leopard murals. Teensy bananas, the variety that causes embarrassment in the produce aisle, were tucked among yellow oncidiums. Dinner included a burlesque show—extra spice for a blushing Midwesterner's birthday.

The dance floor was so crowded that teams of servers in white dinner jackets had to move entire tables to the kitchen. The spontaneity was, truthfully, planned down to the minute.

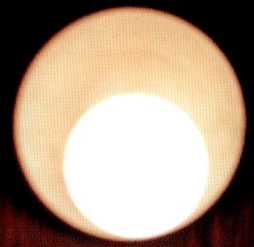

SHE'S GONE COUNTRY

In the Cumberland Gap, a few hours from Knoxville, Tennessee, a young couple celebrated their engagement surrounded by bits and pieces of their families. Whiskey sours were served overlooking the lake and under the watchful eye of a sly fox.

Quilts from both grandmothers dressed the farm tables surrounded by a motley assortment of vintage dining chairs begged and borrowed from nearby antique stores. The incongruous assembly brought warmth and embraced the charm of imperfection. The wildflowers were locally sourced—the heart of the matter.

Guests were transported in yellow school buses to nearby Oaklawn Farms for bull ridin' and boot scootin'. Then, Rodney Atkins popped on stage to sing "Farmer's Daughter."

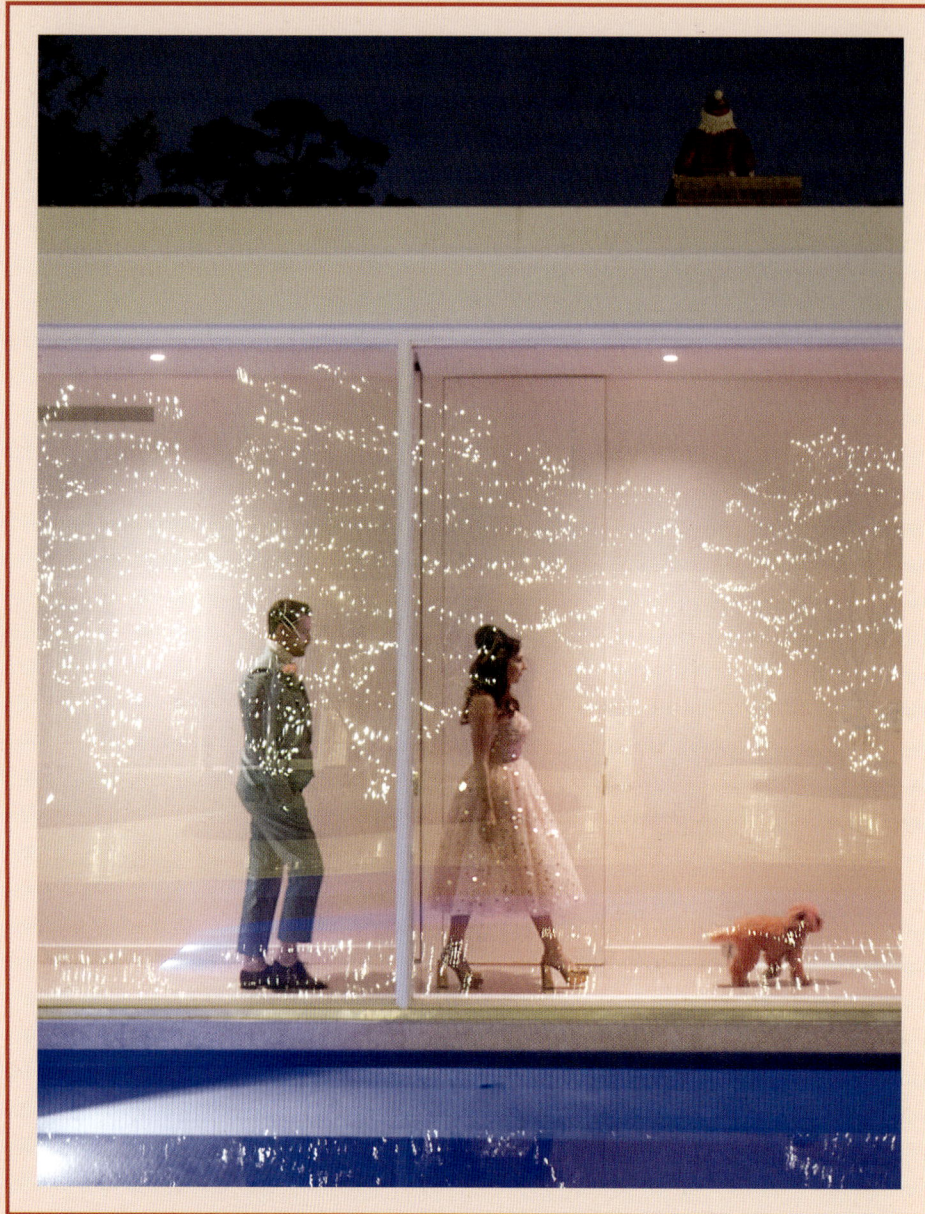

PINK POODLE PARTY

An annual Pink Poodle Party encourages both style and season in Houston each December. The best guests dress. In this case, the flounces of full skirts, kid gloves, and teased bouffants became the decoration.

A Jerry Lee Lewis impersonator played the baby grand as servers passed pigs in a blanket and shrimp cocktail with pearl toothpicks and pink poodle linen napkins made in Madeira, Portugal, just for the occasion. A wonderland of nostalgic desserts was served from the dining room table. I directed servers to offer slices and scoops with smiles as some guests were convinced the buffet was an art installation.

There was a magician, a synchronized-swimming performance, a DJ, and a Bettie Page mermaid splashing in the mint marbled hammam. Sometimes, the house is the party. At midnight, we pulled back the curtains in the living room to reveal a secret dance floor. Then, the real Santa arrived to send guests on their way with festive unnecessaries.

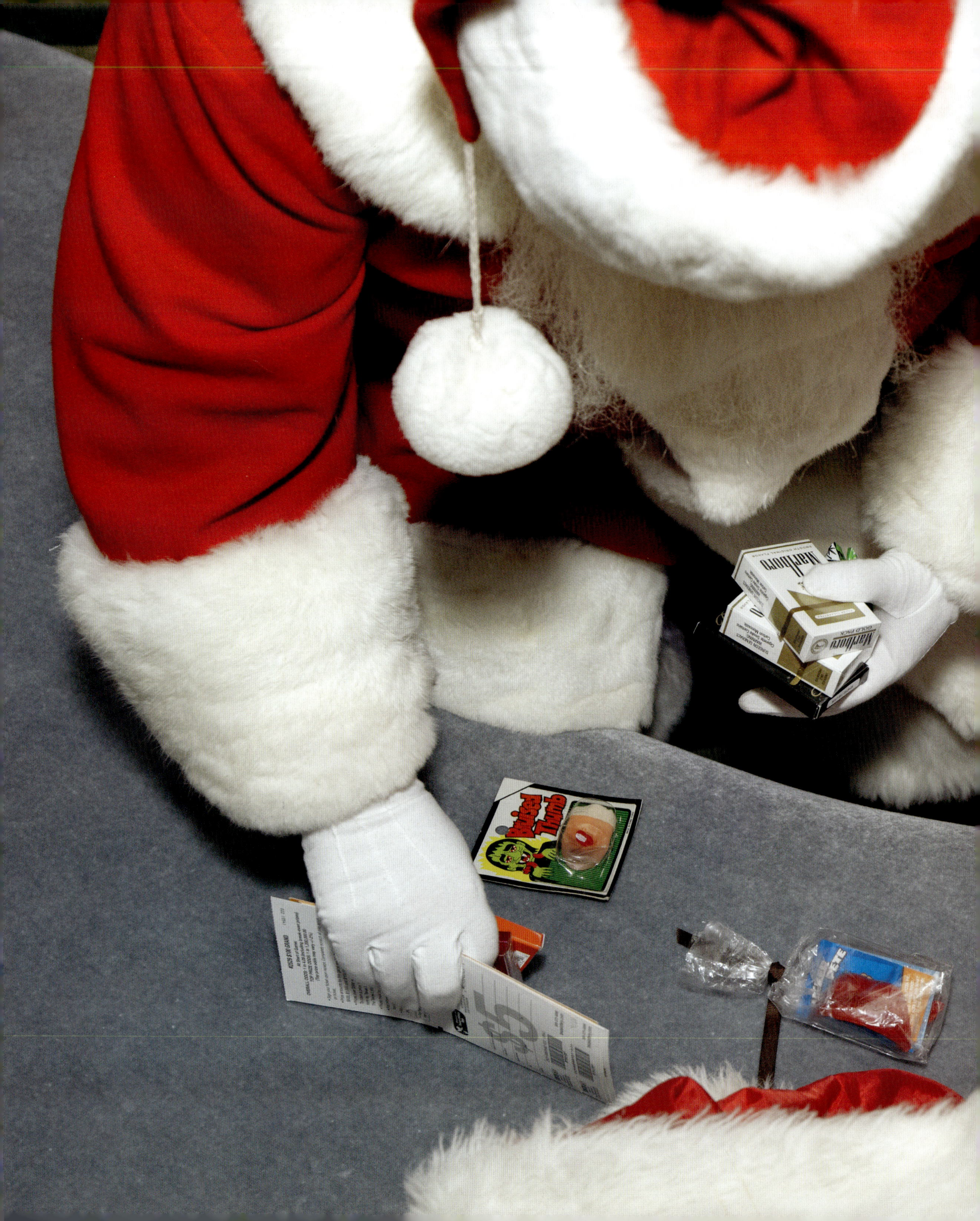

Get Up Offa That Thing

Don't stay in one room all night.

A change of location from cocktails to dinner or dinner to dancing sparks a sense of adventure and momentum.

At a basic human level, moving en masse does something to us physically and spiritually. For proof, look no further than Catholic genuflection, the fever pitch of the hora as the klezmer picks up speed, or the joie de vivre and buckjumping of a New Orleans second line.

If you're bored, so are your guests. Change the music. Change the lighting. Change your outfit. You just redid your bathroom? Fill the bathtub with ice and make it the bar.

When *Elle Decor* featured my one-bedroom Greenwich Village apartment, the article opened with, "She can pack forty happy guests into an apartment 'the size of a nipple.'" Quite the visual but right on the money. People like to come to my apartment because what it lacks in space, it makes up for in style. Besides, the Holly Golightly fantasy is probably what drew them to New York in the first place. I often host eight for dinner in my bedroom on a folding table covered in a custom tablecloth and pulled up to my canopy bed. It's a little weird and a lot of fun, and it all begins the second my guests come through the door, and I tell them to hang their own coat. They open the closet to find that I've turned it into a bar, complete with a uniformed bartender chosen for his slight build, short stature, and ability to hang coats while shaking martinis.

Even when I entertain out and about in New York, I keep it moving. I once invited twenty-four friends to meet me at Caffe Dante on MacDougal and after a negroni, I naively asked if we were ready for dinner. Out the door and around the corner we went to Raffetto's, a small Italian grocery store owned by a friend's family. We pulled barstools up to the shop counter and ate four courses of handmade pasta prepared à la minute, surrounded by neatly stacked cans of San Marzano tomatoes and barrels of oil-cured olives, under an arbor of hanging salumi. As we finished our last bites of chocolate cake, a brass band arrived to push us off of our stools, blasting "Mambo Italiano" as we made our way down Houston to a club in SoHo to tie one on.

Every party needs a Pied Piper. It's usually me, but it can be anyone with charisma who's amenable to assuming the role.

At a welcome party on a riverboat in Ohio, the cute-as-a-button lead singer of the band was a willing partner in whatever I asked, which at one point included pretending we'd been attacked by pirates on a pontoon boat flying a flag that read "What a Catch."

For a wedding in Tennessee, we found one of the actual banjo players from *O Brother, Where Art Thou?* and hired him to usher guests from the ceremony to cocktails.

For a party at Castello di Amorosa, I found a Bacchus who looked every inch the carouser, and as soon as I swapped his mail-order toga for an old muslin sheet from L'Isle-sur-la-Sorgue, he became the god of wine. My only concern was whether the platform where he was splayed out eating grapes would collapse from all the guests climbing up to take selfies, but by the grace of Jupiter, all was well. Instead of closing the bar (tacky), script a grand finale. At the end of the night, Bacchus led the crowd to their hotel shuttles with a wonderfully pitchy rendition of "That's Amore."

If you find yourself without a barman in the closet, a bandleader, a banjo player, or a Bacchus, lean into what you've got. Years ago, I planned a party for friends at their Sears Catalog cottage in Napa, which happened to be on the path of the Napa Valley Wine Train. Cattle bells were passed, and when the train rolled through, guests hurried to the table in the vineyard to hoot and holler, cheering as though the passengers were soldiers returning from war. Dinner is served.

Take turns leading the table in your college fight song. Hire a drag queen to judge a dance-off to "Material Girl." Give New York City Ballet prima ballerinas a reason to dance to '90s rap at the Russian Samovar. Tempt your guests to end the night at your favorite pizzeria and buy a slice for everyone in line. Light one of those gender reveal sticks and start walking in the direction you want everyone to go, leaving a thick trail of pink smoke in your wake. Nothing, absolutely nothing, gets people out of their seats like James Brown and espresso martinis.

The world is your oyster. For my last birthday, I hired a school bus to pick us up from dinner and drive through Times Square blaring Gloria Estefan on the way to a piano bar. People stared, thank God, and the looks on their faces—a cocktail of confusion and delight—felt a lot like love.

TRAVELING SALVATION SHOW

Each spring, the design driven descend on a small strip of Texas farmland for the Round Top Antiques Fair. The excitement of gathering made it a perfect place for Houses & Parties to premier a Traveling Salvation Show of wonder and whimsy. Vagabonds, searching for the next party.

A Barnum & Bailey Circus caravan from the turn of the last century beckoned guests inside the red-and-white-striped circus tent. Tables were tucked under low-hanging painted panels from a 1920s French merry-go-round and rattan hot-air balloons bursting with yellow ranunculus. Antique suzanis hung from the ceiling. Wood shavings were strewn a foot deep across the floor, like at a horse show.

Platters of homemade Texas Hill Country dishes were passed from the beds of nearby pickup trucks. There were mini ham biscuits and old-fashioned recipes made from local ingredients. Even vegetarians like ham biscuits. Parlor games and icebreakers inside marbled-paper party crackers united the willing crowd.

Deep In The H...

The stars at night are...
(clap, clap, clap, clap),
Deep in the hear...
The prairie sky is...
(clap, clap, ...
Deep in the he...

The sage in blooms is like...
(clap, clap, clap, clap),
Deep in the heart of Texas.
Reminds me of the one I love
(clap, clap, clap, clap),
Deep in the heart of Texas.

The coyotes wail along the trail
(clap, clap, clap, clap),
Deep in the heart of Texas.
The rabbits rush around the brush
(clap, clap, clap, clap),
Deep in the heart of Texas.

The cowboys cry, "Ki-yip-pee-yi"
(clap, clap, clap, clap),
Deep in the heart of Texas.
The doggies bawl and bawl and bawl
(clap, clap, clap, clap),
Deep in the heart of Texas.

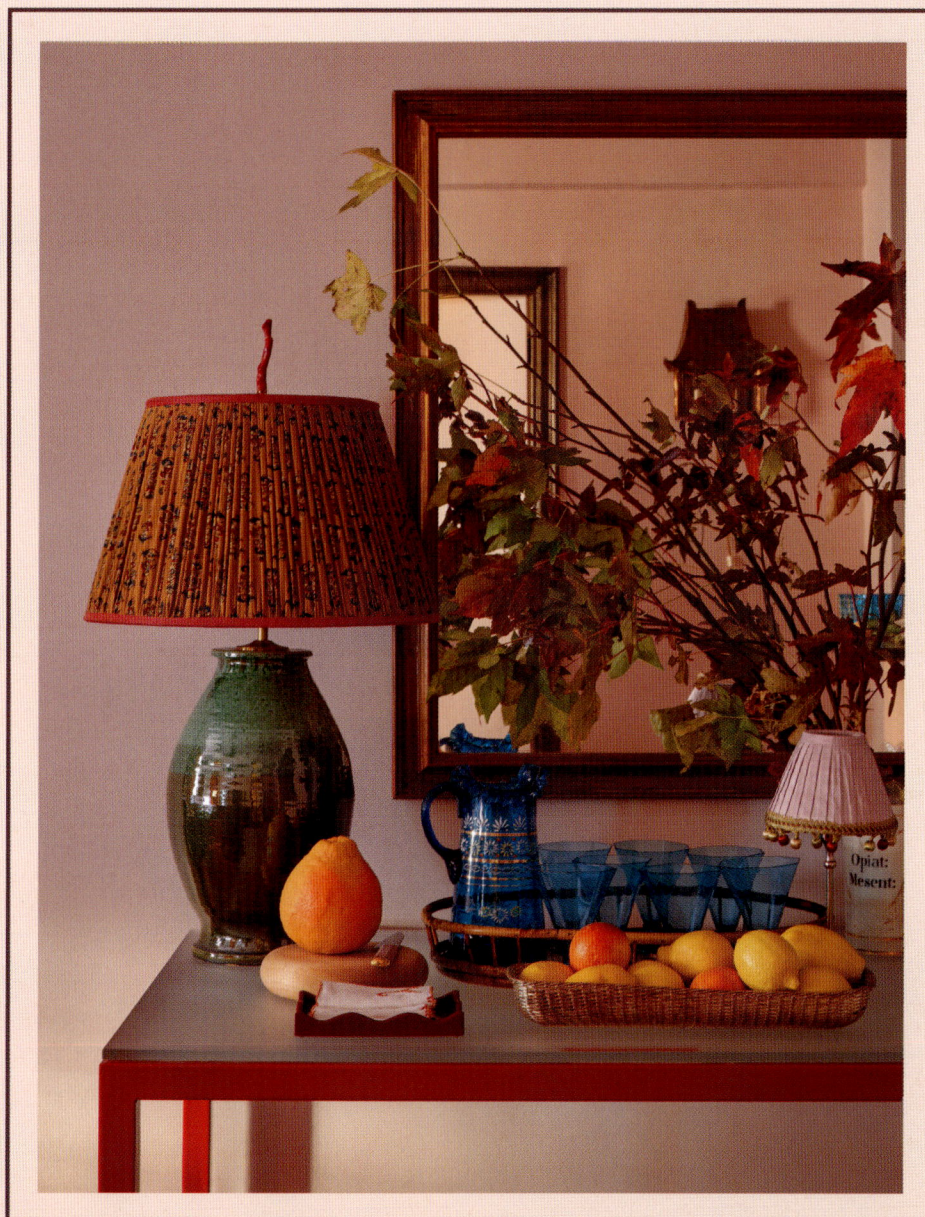

TINY COCKTAILS, TEENY DINNER

My jewel-box apartment in New York is a great place to gather. It's teeny tiny, but I've been known to host fifty for cocktails. I turn the coat closet into a bar just big enough to shake a martini, and I ice champagne in the kitchen sink. The lights are low and spirits are high.

My bedroom is just big enough to set up the eight-foot-long folding table I keep under my bed. I can have ten, tops, for a seated dinner, which is always Mr. Chow delivery served family style right out of the containers. I have lots of standing champagne buckets to hold wine at the foot of the bed, an arm's length from the closet.

Weird, little spaces encourage unexpected fodder, and a party in a bedroom might just end in a competitive game of pass the orange.

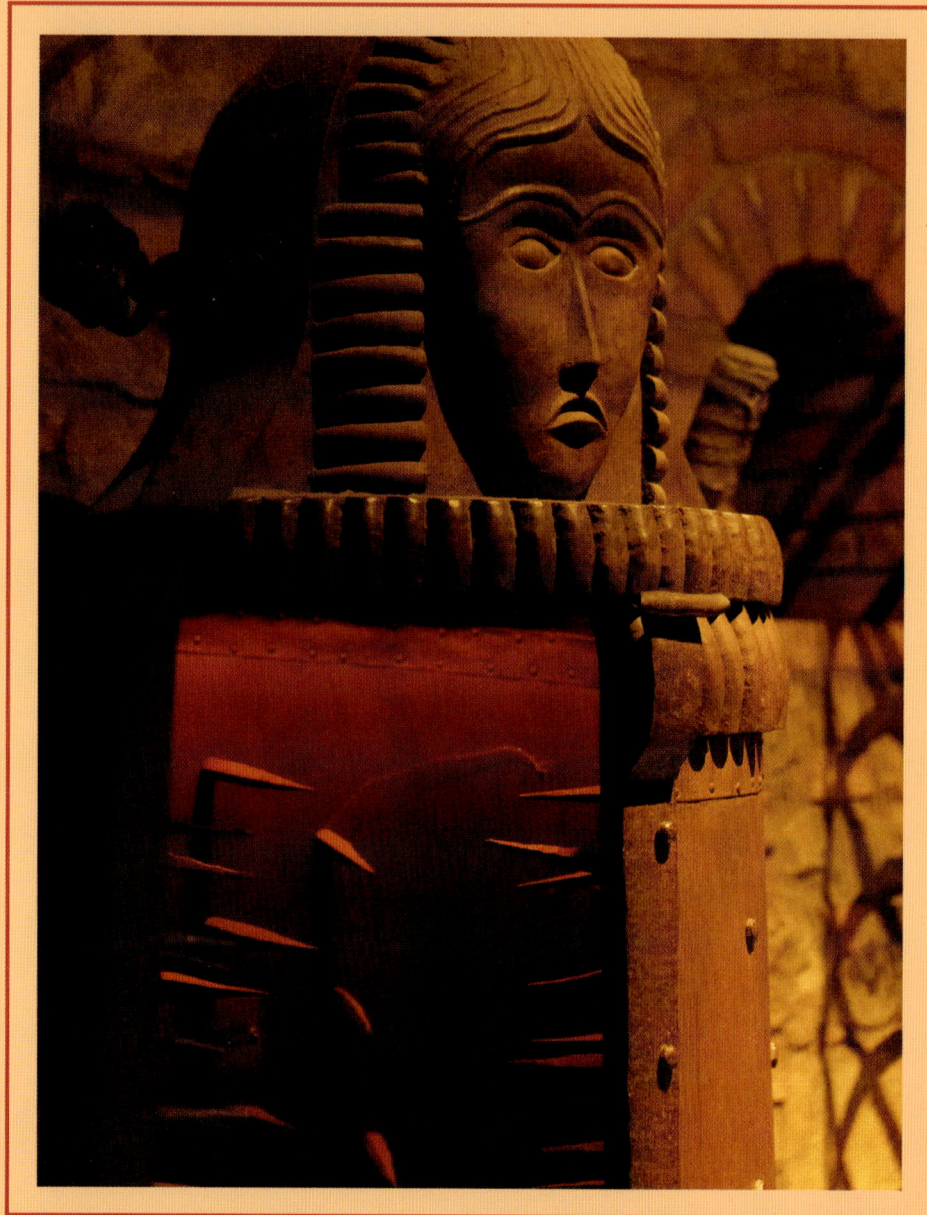

THAT'S AMORE

When I design a party, the venue dictates everything. Castello di Amorosa is a winery in Napa Valley styled as a fourteenth-century Tuscan castle. It has a drawbridge, five towers, a chapel, an armory, and a torture chamber. Now, that's . . . amore.

Two hundred fifty guests gathered in Calistoga-cum-Cortona to celebrate the beginning of a wedding weekend. The party started late, after dinner, and we served local wine and brick oven pizza. No one, ever, turns down a slice of pizza.

A talented Bacchus let me drape him in a scratchy antique linen sheet that had not been washed since 1890. He posed for photos and then led the party in a jubilant rendition of Dean Martin's famous ditty as they walked back over the drawbridge and headed home. Atop a tower with the lighting guys and moved by the effort, I waved a cocktail napkin and screamed "bravo" over and over, pretending to be at La Scala.

Bibbidi-Babbidi-Boo

The phone lit up with a call from Francis Ford Coppola's office. An assistant said that she was connecting me, and then there he was, the great auteur, asking if we could engrave a set of Puiforcat tumblers he'd bought from my store for his daughter, Sofia. Just as I was about to tell him, the call clicked.

A few months later, I was sitting at a West Village haunt with several close friends. Once we had crawled into our cups, I spotted Sofia Coppola and her husband sitting across the room. "Don't do it," they said as I walked over to introduce myself. "Sofia, it's me," I said (as if she knew me). Her husband stood up, radiating a mixture of chivalry and concern. Undeterred, I pressed on. "It's me, Rebecca," I said, taking off my Covid-era surgical mask. It still wasn't registering. "I have a store called Houses & Parties, and I design events." "Oh, yes," she replied. "From down south."

Hours later, I woke for water and Advil and a cringe, pacing and wringing my hands like Lady Macbeth at the thought of embarrassing myself with such bravado. The next week, Sofia's husband called me to plan her fiftieth birthday party. The dinner would be in May in the courtyard of their townhouse in the West Village, and the creative brief would remain a surprise.

We got to work making pink cotton-twill table skirts with a gathered ball gown silhouette poufed by four layers of crinoline petticoat so that when guests pulled up a chair, they'd become berries plopped into Chantilly cream. I shipped sterling and all the china (hand-painted French porcelain featuring fruits, flowers, mushrooms, and insects) from Savannah. The glassware was from Saint-Louis, the oldest crystal blowers in the world, which made for a hold-your-breath boxing-and-unboxing process. Overhead, I hung pale orange silk Chinese lanterns I bought in San Francisco, outfitted with pink lightbulbs and crimson silk tassels from Samuel & Sons. The pleated shades on the table lamps were yet another pink, and the net effect of so many sherbet tones was more mood than color.

I ironed hemstitched napkins, folded them into envelopes that held the menu cards (a Martha Stewart trick), added another silk tassel, and I then scattered the table with lychee in sterling Cartier baskets and ceramic insects with wire legs. The pink peonies were left out in the sun, and by late afternoon, they were leaning toward one another like cool girls, even softer than they looked.

When Sofia saw the courtyard, she gasped. I told her I was inspired by her Tina Barney photographs. "I think it's more Danielle Steel . . . in Dallas." Well, I'll take it.

VISIONS OF SUGARPLUMS

Christmas is my favorite holiday. It's full of nostalgia and excitement and dressy parties. I hosted a small group for an early supper before everyone scattered for the holidays. Tables were set in the hallway and then quickly removed for the next wave of guests—a second invitation on the same night for a cocktail bash. Stacking parties maximizes effort and the night ends with "come one, come all" merriment.

I invited one hundred guests, hoping for sixty, and got ninety. Two big bars kept everyone smiling as servers passed simple and delicious cocktail fare. A towering fantasy of sweets included decorated sugar cookies, gas station Hostess Sno Balls, a big coconut cake, and fancy candy collected on my travels from Fortnum & Mason to Marchesi 1824. This is my mother's trick. She spent hours meticulously piping fir wreaths around the necks of pink pigs and mixed them with grocery store iced animal cookies surrounding a big punch bowl of eggnog. More is merrier.

As the night ended, I bribed surly teenagers with wads of cash to wrangle children for caroling on the stairs.

Anatomy of the Party

Events are live theater. There will be surprises. Plan every minute on paper so that you—and anyone you've enlisted to help—stay on track and can quickly regroup when distracted. I even make a run of show for myself when I have a small dinner party so that I can drink wine and have fun and remember to take the roast out of the oven. Other than that, here are a few considerations for excellence.

INVITATIONS: There's always a reason to celebrate; put it on the invitation. Guests will know who to thank, who to congratulate, what to toast, and how to dress. (Note that "black tie optional" is not a clear option.) This makes everyone feel at ease. I like almost everything old-fashioned, including fancy engraved invitations on toothy paper or with hand-painted edges, especially on pearl-white cards so thick you could use them as shingles. Weddings always call for a printed invite. But I embrace digital invitations for many occasions and the opportunity for playful

moving images, hysterical collages, and helpful tracking options. A thoughtful text can translate to a festive but kicked-back Saturday night, no pressure.

VENUE: When choosing a venue, think about how the moments will transition. Baby kissing to brunch to shower. Cocktails to dinner to dancing. Toasts to dessert to flash mob. Parties can last for several hours. You don't want to be in one room all night. It's better to have an enfilade for a change of scenery. I prefer quirky and unexpected locations that no one has dared to explore, places that are accessible and yet transcend the mundane. A luncheon in the greenhouse among the annuals at your local nursery. A dinner in the back of a flatbed trailer that drives around the neighborhood lit with Christmas lights. A private disco at the roller rink with a catered cocktail buffet positioned far away from shoe cubbies.

GUEST LIST: Devoting time to making new and interesting friends is an honorable

UNIVERSAL
WINE

DINNER
(HANDWASH)

WATER
(WO ICE)

DUMPLINGS

CHOCOLATE SAUCE

ICE CREAM

pursuit that will serve you well. It's more fun to have a mix of people of different backgrounds and ages—and with different personalities and fascinations. I tend to host and encourage guest lists that are either very exclusive or very inclusive. Landing in the middle can hurt feelings and inhibit the pursuit of popularity.

DECOR: Make a little world for your guests by considering the ceiling, walls, and floor. Canopies, tree branches, and even string lights make spaces cozy. Build a forest and hang lanterns low so that guests can tuck into an adventure. Cover the walls in yards of generously bunched pink silk or hang beaded curtains for a tease. Save bags of raked leaves to dump on the floor for an underfoot fall crunch.

TABLETOP: A seated affair calls for silver cream and spray starch. Choose your best linens—place mats or a tablecloth but preferably not place mats on a tablecloth. I hope you already know where the forks go. Use luncheon napkins for dinner and soup spoons for dessert. No one (except maybe your mother-in-law) cares, as long as it's attractive and functional. When hosting a big group, print menu cards. I use menu cards as place cards and write the names of my guests at the top. I have lots of ideas for parlor games, but sometimes you just need a little gossipy piece of folded paper like a note passed in math class. "Ask John about his nipple rings." The further from the truth, the better. When you think you're done, add one more element that is just for fodder.

LIGHTING: Often overlooked, lighting is of utmost importance. Avoid direct overhead lights like the plague. Keep the lights low. Modern lighting systems rarely allow for adequate dimming. You have to cut the lights and place candles at varying heights: candelabra, candlesticks, votives. Buy twelve-hour votives (that really only last five hours) and dripless wax tapers (that only drip a little). Cheap paper doilies make great bobeches if their frill is right for your look. Table lamps with silk shades cast a flattering glow, and I love anything pierced that creates dappled light. I often use wicker lampshades for this reason. Change the mood throughout the evening. You want the light bright enough that everyone swoons over the flowers and knows what they're eating, but it should be turned way down for dessert and certainly for dancing.

FLOWERS: You can have a party without flowers; swap them for masses of candles, potted ferns, or bouquets of balloons. But flowers are unrivaled in beauty and indulgence. My favorite are Iceland poppies, which twist and turn and flatter negative space. Like all the best women, they are expensive and fickle. Tulips are a challenge and better single in bud vases. They are unruly and flop with the slightest change of temperature. They also grow after they are cut—a lot. I like flowers that mind. When I arrange flowers myself, for either my house or smaller parties, I stick to one kind and give them lots of breathing room for asymmetry and imperfection. It's best to leave mixed, ambitious arrangements to the professionals brussels sprouts

and smart to request bits of ugly. Think weird colors, wicked textures. If something is too pretty, it's not interesting. Plan ahead with lots of inspiration images. Flowers are perishable, and the florist needs to be inside your head to effectively pivot in case a crop arrives at the wholesaler in sad shape. Vessels can make or break any effort, and please keep them low so your guests can see across the table. Baskets, cachepots, Venetian tumblers, or mounds of chicken wire covered in sheet moss are all superior to a square pressed glass vase. We all know where the devil lives, so don't forget to scatter single blooms across the tablecloth.

MENU: When planning a menu for a party, avoid haute cuisine. Guests appreciate simple, delicious food more than complicated foams and silly garnishes. Anticipate dietary restrictions by providing lots of options. My formula includes a substantial protein, a sinful starch, something green and fresh, a second vegetable dish, and a decadent dessert.

Remember, outsourcing preserves the personality you will need for guests.

I like to pass a strong cocktail as guests enter a party so that everyone loosens up. Cosmos (more vodka, less triple sec) and margaritas (I like Jean-Georges's Ginger Margarita) batch well. I also serve Earl Grey–Bourbon Punch to a crowd. I use a recipe from *Bon Appétit* and substitute with Lapsang Souchong. Beyond that, I'm not a fan of signature cocktails. Too sweet. You should have choices. I advocate for a full bar (vodka, tequila, gin, and bourbon are just fine) with white wine and a festive option for those not imbibing. Delicious and simple options include iced green tea, Topo Chico with bitters, or a Mexican Coke on cracked ice with lemon.

These are just a few elements of a successful party. But really, your only obligation as a host is to be thoughtful and generous when considering the comfort of your guests and the delicate trade of their time and your effort.

RESOURCES

HOUSES & PARTIES
Tabletop, offbeat gifts, party hats, entertainments, home
housesandparties.com
Savannah, Georgia, and
New York City

INVITATIONS

ASHLEY CURRY
Classic hand calligraphy
ashleycurry.com
Savannah, Georgia

BERNARD MAISNER
Fanciful hand calligraphy and lettering
bernardmaisner.com
New York City

CAITLIN MCGAULEY
Painted illustrations
caitlinmcgauley.com
New York City

CHEREE BERRY PAPER & DESIGN
Full-service design studio
chereeberrypaperdesign.com
St. Louis, Missouri

DEAR ANNABELLE
Ready-to-write and bespoke stationery
dearannabelle.com
New York City

DEMPSEY & CARROLL
Classic engraved invitations
dempseyandcarroll.com
New York City

EMBOSSED GRAPHICS OF TEXAS
Design and engraving printer
graphics@egotpress.com
Houston

HAPPY MENOCAL
Illustrator with creative think tank
happymenocal.com
Bedford, New York

HiNOTE
Playful invitations for texting
hinoteapp.com
San Francisco

SMYTHSON
Classic engraved invitations
smythson.com
London

STEPHANIE FISHWICK
Illustrator with full-service design
stephaniefishwick.com
Charlottesville, Virginia

STICKER PLANET
Every sticker in your dreams
stickerplanet.com
Los Angeles

MENU

À LA MÈRE DE FAMILLE
Chocolates and novelty marzipan
lameredefamille.com
Paris

BLUE BELL CREAMERIES
Simply the best ice cream
bluebell.com
Brenham, Texas

THE BUTTER END
Sculpted cakes with masterful decorations
thebutterend.com
Santa Monica and Gardena, California

CALLIE'S HOT LITTLE BISCUIT
Country ham biscuits for cocktails
calliesbiscuits.com
Charleston, South Carolina

CAROLINE'S CAKES
7-Layer Caramel Cake
carolinescakes.com
Spartanburg, South Carolina

THE CAVIAR CO.
The country's best caviar
thecaviarco.com
San Francisco

CHARLOTTE NEUVILLE CAKES AND CONFECTIONS
Extraordinary cakes
charlotteneuvillecakes.com
New York City

THE FAB FÊTE
Frozen souffles
thefabfete.com
Houston

FLORIDA STONE CRAB
Jumbo crab claws
flstonecrab.com
Hudson, Florida

FORTNUM & MASON
Wonderful display of unusual sweets
fortnumandmason.com
London

FUNNY FACE BAKERY
Hysterical portrait cookies
funnyfacebakery.com
New York City

GOODE CO.
Brazos Bottom Pecan Pies
goodecompany.com
Houston

JEN MONROE
Chef, artist, and food designer
badtaste.biz
New York City

MARCHESI 1824
Fancy candy
marchesi1824.com
Milan and London

MILES OF CHOCOLATE
Decadent ganache brownies
milesofchocolate.com
Austin, Texas

OKAMOTO STUDIO CUSTOM ICE
Masterful ice sculptures
okamotostudionyc.com
New York City

OTTOLENGHI
Cookbooks full of party ideas
ottolenghi.co.uk
London

THE ROUNDS
Tiny cookies, sweet and savory
theroundsnyc.com
Brooklyn, New York

SISTER SCHUBERT'S
Parker House Style Yeast Rolls, forever
sisterschuberts.com
Columbus, Ohio

WILLIAM POLL
Watercress Dip for tea sandwiches
williampoll.com
New York City

CATERING

GLORIOUS FOOD
Delicious food with elegant service, my go-to
gloriousfood.com
New York City

GOODNIGHT HOSPITALITY
Limitless imagination and impeccable execution
goodnighthospitality.com
Houston

KB TABLE
An excellent collaborator
kbtable.com
Austin, Texas

PAULA LEDUC FINE CATERING & EVENTS
Eye-popping presentations
paulaleduc.com
Emeryville, California

RED KAP
Classic bartender jackets
redkap.com
Nashville, Tennessee

TABLETOP & DECOR

BBJ LA TAVOLA
Linen rentals, Nuovo solid is my favorite
bbjlatavola.com
Niles, Illinois

BIZ STAIN ELIMINATOR
Care for fine linens
bizstainfighter.com

BROOKLYN BALLOON COMPANY
Balloon creations
brooklynballoon company.com
Brooklyn, New York

COURTLAND & CO.
Custom monograms and fine linens
courtlandandco.com
Savannah, Georgia

KRB NYC
Objects of charm for houses and parties
krbnyc.com
New York City

MIDORI
Luxurious silk ribbon
midoriribbon.com
Los Angeles

PRINT APPEAL
Custom printed paper goods
printappeal.com
Dallas

SAMUEL & SONS
Sumptuous passementerie
samuelandsons.com
New York City

TOY JOY
Buckets of plastic snails and the like
toyjoy.com
Austin, Texas

WRIGHT'S SILVER CREAM
No substitute
jawright.com
Gurnee, Illinois

FLOWERS

BLOSSOMS EVENTS
Makers of flowers and large-scale dreams
blossomsevents.com
Murrells Inlet, South Carolina

DUTCH FLOWER LINE
Resource for the finest cut flowers
nyfg.nyc
New York City

EMILY THOMPSON FLOWERS
Otherworldly flowers and installations
emilythompsonflowers.com
New York City

FOX FODDER FARM
Flowers with perfect peculiar tension, my go-to
foxfodderfarm.com
New York City

ISA ISA
Foraged, emotive, and colorful
isafloral.com
Los Angeles

KALAPANA TROPICALS
Exotic orchids
kalapanatropicals.com
Kurtistown, Hawaii

KATHLEEN DEERY DESIGN
Beautiful and sensuous arrangements
kathleendeerydesign.com
Emeryville, California

MCQUEENS FLOWERS
Timeless blooms at all scales
mcqueensflowers.com
London

NIWAKI
Sakagen Flower Scissors
niwaki.com
Shaftesbury and London

THE PETALER
Uptown funk and festive
thepetalerfloralandeventsco.com
Houston

RENKO FLORAL
Just the wildest and wonderful
renkofloral.com
Los Angeles and Honolulu

ROSE STORY FARM
Heirloom roses
rosestoryfarm.com
Carpinteria, California

BIG PARTIES

LEVY NYC
Cutting-edge event lighting
levynyc.net
New York City

MCCOY'S EVENT PROFESSIONALS
Event production and Sperry Tents
mccoyseventprofessionals.com

PREMIER SOUND AND LIGHTING
Production and entertainment
premiersoundandlighting.com
Houston

ROSE BRAND
Stage curtains and theatrical fabrics
rosebrand.com
Secaucus, New Jersey

SMASH ENTERTAINMENT
Unique performing talent
smashnyc.com
New York City

SPERRY TENTS
The original sailcloth tents
sperrytents.com

TECHNICAL EVENT COMPANY
Creative lighting and sound production
technicaleventcompany.com
Charleston, South Carolina

TURNIPBLOOD BLACK TIE
Entertainment booking agent
turnipbloodblacktie.com
Nashville, Tennessee

THE VILLAGERS BRASS BAND
The ultimate Pied Pipers
Instagram.com/thevillagersnyc
New York City

COMPLIMENTS

Before I took an apartment in New York, I came across Derek Blasberg in the contributor pages of *Harper's Bazaar* and decided that he would be my boyfriend. I didn't know him—or that he already had a boyfriend. I invited him to SCAD to speak to creative-writing students, and we became good friends because we're both funny and he's kind. Years later, when I was starting my own business, Houses & Parties, he said I should talk to his friend Lauren Santo Domingo, who has plenty of both. She had recently launched her glamorous online luxury retailer, Moda Operandi, and all eyes were watching her smart and stylish moves. The three of us met for lunch at Amaranth during New York Fashion Week. They were late and both ordered lasagna. Lauren said she'd love to have a party at her house in Water Mill and asked if I had any ideas. I riffed, saying something about pots of French strawberries all down the table, and it was settled. They left after a few bites, and I sat surrounded by full plates, alive to possibility.

That meeting, and the clients Lauren and Derek graciously sent my way, were indelible strokes of good fortune and generosity. I cannot imagine more influential endorsements or loyal supporters to jump-start my adventure.

A great deal of my value is in my relationships, both personal and professional. There are so many people who made this book possible and continue to bring talent and enthusiasm to a tenacious pursuit of gathering, beauty, and unabashed joy.

These colleagues and friends join forces to dream, make, and execute all that Houses & Parties offers to devotees of the elegant and unusual. I am immensely grateful to work alongside these shooting stars who have helped me in ways only partially illustrated in this book.

Adam Kuehl was the principal photographer for this book and captures all the Houses & Parties magic (including our insane retail photo shoots). Our brains are so well acquainted, they have their own language grounded in hums, grunts, and knowing smiles. I trust only Adam with the impossible

task of capturing fleeting moments, subtle tensions, twisted humor, mixed emotions, and excruciating detail in single images.

Kimberlin Rogers is the director of events at Houses & Parties. All the work in these pages was executed under her stylish spell. Kimberlin exhibits all the attributes of the bravest firemen: integrity, fitness, versatility, dedication, and leadership. She can make a bourbon snowball in hell wearing pressed linen.

Andrea Slaven runs all three offices, and her hand has remained steady on my shoulder for almost a decade. She's the great motivator with a prudent business head. I credit any success to the peace of mind that Andrea's expertise, loyalty, and advice enables.

A deep curtsy to Sophie Uribe, who leads the interior design office, and Colby Goetschius, who leads the retail office of Houses & Parties. We know that a house is a party is a house is an . . . online shopping destination.

Taylor Patterson of Fox Fodder Farm can translate language into flowers with the intention and precision of a poet. Her work shines in these photographs. When I start a project, I call her first.

Trish Andersen, a magic maker extraordinaire, conjures the wacky, weird, and wonderful. She once installed thirty-foot-tall paper palm trees that appeared to be growing from a bed of paper caladium misted with Clorox to mimic sunspots.

Emily Testa is an exceptional writer and taskmaster. We've been friends for decades, which is why it is fun.

Kravet granted me the honor of using prints from Lee Jofa, Brunschwig & Fils, and Donghia as part of this book's design. The house in my head is completely covered in their rosy Katibi print, curtains to crapaud (it now serves as the endpapers of this book). I scour their showrooms sourcing the prints and patterns that make my events, interiors, and e-commerce collections full of substance and style.

Amy Weinstein at Smash Entertainment is Charlie, and her talented angels add the surprising and quirky and weird. She's sourced absolutely everything from baskets of albino bunnies to the real Santa—in April.

Lindsey Huttenbauer is a trusted collaborator and events comrade. Lindsey puts all the pieces together and could just as easily run the National Airspace System.

Meg Connolly Communications waves their wand in my direction almost every day. Especially Meg, who sits on my shoulder, closest to my ear.

Sarah Stump, at Rizzoli, had the vision for this book and the enthusiasm of a cheerleader. I am equally thankful for both.

Finally, I offer deep appreciation to my clients, who allowed me the opportunity to make little worlds and create celebrations for their memories.

First published in the United States of America in 2025 by
Rizzoli International Publications, Inc.
49 West 27th Street
New York, NY 10001
www.rizzoliusa.com

PUBLISHER: Charles Miers
EDITOR: Sarah Stump
DESIGN: Celia Fuller
PRODUCTION MANAGER: Colin Hough Trapp
MANAGING EDITOR: Lynn Scrabis
COPY EDITOR: Susan Homer
PROOFREADER: Candice Fehrman

ISBN: 978-0-8478-7425-5
Library of Congress Control Number: 2025932913

FSC
www.fsc.org
MIX
Paper | Supporting
responsible forestry
FSC® C104723

Printed in China
2025 2026 2027 2028 / 10 9 8 7 6 5 4 3 2

The authorized representative in the EU for
product safety and compliance is
Mondadori Libri S.p.A., via Gian Battista Vico 42, Milan,
Italy, 20123, www.mondadori.it

Visit us online:
Instagram.com/RizzoliBooks
Facebook.com/RizzoliNewYork
Youtube.com/user/RizzoliNY

IMAGE CREDITS

All photography by Adam Kuehl except:

Pages 7, 8–9, 229: William Laird; Pages 38, 39, 42, 46,
106, 110 (top left and bottom left), 111, 113, 117, 123,
174–177, 181, 182–183, 217, 220, 226–227, 240–241,
243 (top right): Courtesy of Houses & Parties

Cover: Jonathan Adler for Kravet, Acid Palm;
Pages 2, 85–103, 252: Greenacres Arts Center; Pages
4, 53–61: Night Gallery; Pages 4, 53–55, 60–61: Jason
Hackenworth; Page 17: The Nomad Band; Pages 22–23:
Napa Valley Wine Train; Pages 24–37: The Russian
Samovar; Pages 28 (top right and bottom left), 37, 100:
Smash Party Entertainment; Pages 39–49: Beaulieu
Garden; Pages 62–71: BB Riverboats; Pages 66–67, 111:
Turnipblood Entertainment; Page 75: Brass Animals;
Pages 90, 101: Jordan Kahn Music Company; Pages 107,
108–109: Rockin A Mules; Pages 112, 122: DailyDish
Events & Catering; Pages 128–131: Le Gratin; Pages
132–133: La Chiva Loca Party Bus; Pages 136–145:
Vibrant; Pages 139, 143, 144–145: Jackson & Company;
Pages 146–152: Aiken-Rhett House Museum, c. 1820s,
Historic Charleston Foundation, for Charleston by
Design, 2023; Pages 155, 192–193: J&D Entertainment;
Pages 164–173: El Tucán; Pages 182–183: Oaklawn
Farms; Pages 186–187: ©2024 Amoako Boafo /
Licensed by Artists Rights Society (ARS), New York;
Pages 190–191: Aqualillies, the world's premier artistic
swimming performance company; Pages 216–227:
Castello di Amorosa; Pages 222–223: Élan Artists

REBECCA GARDNER is the founder and creative director of Houses & Parties, an events, interior design, and retail collective based in New York and Savannah, Georgia. She has been named a top event designer by *Vogue* and *Harper's Bazaar*. Her design work and advice on entertaining have been published in *The Wall Street Journal*, *Architectural Digest*, *T Magazine*, *Elle Decor*, *Town & Country*, *Financial Times*, and *House Beautiful*. And her online shop (**housesandparties.com**) offers unnecessaries for devotees of the elegant and unusual.

ADAM KUEHL has collaborated with Rebecca Gardner for eighteen years. His photography has been exhibited internationally and has appeared in publications including *The New York Times*, *Architectural Digest*, *Vogue*, and *National Geographic Traveler*, as well as previous Rizzoli titles *Little Black Dress* and *Oscar de la Renta: His Legendary World of Style*.